Creative Art & Activities

Print Making

Mary Mayesky

THOMSON

DELMAR LEARNING

Australia   Canada   Mexico   Singapore   Spain   United Kingdom   United States

P9-BIP-067

Creative Art and Activities: Print Making
Mary Mayesky

Vice President, Career Ed SBU:
Dawn Gerrain

Director of Editorial:
Sherry Gomoll

Acquisitions Editor:
Erin O'Connor

Developmental Editor:
Alexis Ferraro

Editorial Assistant:
Ivy Ip

Director of Production:
Wendy A. Troeger

Production Coordinator:
Nina Tucciarelli

Composition:
Stratford Publishing Services

Director of Marketing:
Donna J. Lewis

Cover Design:
Tom Cicero

COPYRIGHT © 2004 by Delmar Learning.
A division of Thomson Learning, Inc. Thomson
Learning ™ is a trademark used herein under
license.

Printed in Canada
1 2 3 4 5 XXX 07 06 05 04 03

For more information contact
Delmar Learning,
5 Maxwell Drive,
Clifton Park, NY 12065-2919
at http://www.EarlyChildEd.delmar.com

ALL RIGHTS RESERVED. No part of this work covered by the copyright hereon may be reproduced
or used in any form or by any means—graphic,
electronic, or mechanical, including photocopy-
ing, recording, taping, Web distribution, or information storage and retrieval systems—without
written permission of the publisher.

For permission to use material from this text or
product, contact us by
Tel (800) 730-2214
Fax (800) 730-2215
www.thomsonrights.com

Library of Congress Cataloging-in-Publication
Data

Mayesky, Mary

1-4018-3477-9

NOTICE TO THE READER

Publisher does not warrant or guarantee any of the products described herein or perform any independent analysis in connection with any of the product information contained herein. Publisher does not assume, and expressly disclaims, any obligation to obtain and include information other than that provided to it
by the manufacturer.

The reader is expressly warned to consider and adopt all safety precautions that might be indicated by the activities herein and to avoid all potential hazards. By
following the instructions contained herein, the reader willingly assumes all risks in connection with such instructions.

The Publisher makes no representation or warranties of any kind, including but not limited to, the warranties of fitness for particular purpose or merchantabil-
ity, nor are any such representations implied with respect to the material set forth herein, and the publisher takes no responsibility with respect to such material. The publisher shall not be liable for any special, consequential, or exemplary damages resulting, in whole or part, from the readers' use of, or reliance upon,
this material.

To Kaye,

thank you for being Lucy's very special mother.

With love, Mary

Contents

INTRODUCTION vii

GETTING STARTED vii

    Process vs. Product vii

    Considering the Child viii

    Gathering Materials viii

    Storing and Making Materials Available viii

    Identifying Print-Making Materials x

    Using Food Products x

    Employing Safe Materials x

    Creating a Child-Friendly Environment xi

    Creating a Child's Art Environment xii

    Starting to Collect xii

ACTIVITIES

    ABCs and 123s 1

    Apple Prints 2

    Background Paper Experiments 3

    Berry Nice Prints 4

    Bubble Prints 5

    Can-Top Prints 6

    Cardboard or Rubber Block Prints 7

    Cardboard Relief Prints 8

    Circle Challenge 9

    Cloth Prints 10

    Cork Prints 11

    Crayon Prints 12

    Crayon Shavings Prints 13

    Creative Shoe Prints 14

    Dip It! 15

    Finger Paint Prints 16

    Finger Prints 17

    First Experiments with Monoprints 18

    Glue and Leaf Prints 19

    Great Balls of Fun! 20

    Hair's the Thing 21

    Hand and Foot Prints 22

ACTIVITIES *continued*

Kitchen Prints 23

Monoprints One More Time! 24

Monoprints—Even One More Way! 25

Nature Spatter Prints 26

Paint Monoprints 27

Pasta Prints 28

Pine Cone Prints 29

Play Dough Prints 30

Plunge into It! 31

Print All Over—Body Part Prints 32

Printing Stamps 33

Recycled Puzzle Prints 34

Sandpaper Rubbings 35

Spatter Prints on Fabric 36

Sponge Prints 37

Spray Prints 38

Stick Prints 39

Styrofoam Tray Prints 40

Texture Prints 41

Try These—Experiments with Color 42

Try These—Experiments with Pattern 43

Vegetable Prints 44

Weed Prints 45

What Can It Be? 46

Wheelies! 47

Wood-Block and String Prints 48

Yarn Prints 49

INDEX BY AGES 51

Introduction

Welcome to the world of print making! You will see from the activities in this book that print making is more than just a traditional art activity. Print making is an art form.

Long before they enter the classroom, most children have already discovered their footprints or handprints, made as they walk or play in snow, water, or wet sand. This is why printing with objects is an art activity that is appropriate for the age, ability, and interest level of young preschool children. In a basic printing activity, the child learns that an object dipped in or brushed with paint makes its own mark, or print, on paper. Children use small muscles in the hand, wrist, and fingers as they hold the object, dip it in paint, and print with it on paper. They learn that each object has its own unique quality, that each thing makes its own imprint.

While traditional forms of print making, like stick prints and vegetable prints, are found in this book, also included are such things as bottle caps, Styrofoam, tree bark, stones, and weeds. Once you start print making using these types of materials, you will be encouraged to find many other unique kinds of print making materials.

The activities in this book are designed for children ages 2 through 8. An icon representing a suggested age for the activity is listed at the top of each activity. However, use your own knowledge of the child's abilities to guide you in choosing and using the activities in this book. Wherever appropriate, information is provided on how to adapt the activity for children over age 8.

The focus of this book is creative print making. The activities are meant to be starting points for exploring this art form. Both you and the children are encouraged to explore, experiment, and enjoy the world of print making.

GETTING STARTED

Process vs. Product

The focus of this book and all early childhood art activities is the process, not the product. This means that the process of creating, not the product, is the main reason for the activity. The joys of creating, exploring materials, and discovering how things look and work are all part of the creative process. How the product looks, what it is "supposed to be," is unimportant to the child, and it should be unimportant to the adult.

Young children delight in the experience, the exploration, and the experimentation of art activities. The adult's role is to provide interesting materials and an environment that encourages children's creativity. Stand back when you are tempted to "help" children in their print making. Instead, encourage all children to discover their own unique abilities.

In their first attempts at print making, young children usually work randomly. This is the first step in print making: exploring the media. As children become more and more involved with printing, they develop better understandings of the process and possibilities for various designs.

Some ways to introduce print making activities to children are to:

- Have the children observe and discuss examples of repeat design in clothing, wrapping paper, and wallpaper in which objects appear again and again, up and down, across the material.
- When children are print making, talk about how the children can repeat designs across the material.
- Talk about how an object must be painted each time it is printed.
- Encourage children to experiment with various objects and techniques.

Gradually, through their printing experiences, children discover:

- The amount of paint needed to obtain clean edges
- The amount of pressure needed to get a print
- How the shape and texture of an object determines the shape and texture of the print
- How to repeat a print to create a design

Encourage children to search for objects from the home. Such household items as kitchen utensils, hardware, discarded materials, and many objects of nature are great printing materials. Gradually, children learn to look and discover textures, colors, and patterns all around.

Considering the Child

Young children often find it hard to wait patiently to use materials in an activity. Often, the excitement of creativity and patience do not mix. In addition, it is sometime difficult for young children to share. With young children, plan to have enough print-making materials for each child. For example, having enough sponge shapes so that each child can print without waiting encourages creative print making.

Gathering Materials

Each activity in this book includes a list of required materials. It is important that you gather all materials before starting the activity with children. Children's creative experiences are easily discouraged when they must sit and wait while the adult looks for the tape, extra scissors, or colored paper. Be sure to have the materials gathered in a place the children can easily access.

Storing and Making Materials Available

Having the materials for print making is not enough. These materials must be stored and readily available to the children. For example, scraps of printing materials bunched in a paper bag discourages children from using them. Storing those materials in a clear-plastic box that is shallow enough for children to easily search works much better. Storing small printing items in a recycled muffin tin or even in a fishing box with lots of compartments keeps these supplies orderly and encourages their use. Many teachers find clear-plastic shoe boxes invaluable for storing all the printing objects children use. Such boxes, great for storing and stacking all kinds of art materials, are available at economy stores. **Figure 1** gives more storage ideas.

FIGURE 1 · TIPS FOR STORING ART MATERIALS

The ways materials, supplies, and space are arranged can make or break children's and teachers' art experiences. Following are suggestions for arranging supplies for art experiences:

1. *Scissor holders*. Holders can be made from gallon milk or bleach containers. Simply punch holes in the containers and place scissors in the holes with the scissor points to the inside. Egg cartons turned upside down with slits in each mound also make excellent holders.

2. *Paint containers*. Containers can range from muffin tins and plastic egg cartons to plastic soft-drink cartons with baby food jars in them. These work especially well outdoors as well as indoors, because they are large and not easily tipped. Place one brush in each container. This prevents colors from mixing and makes cleanup easier.

3. *Crayon containers*. Juice and vegetable cans painted or covered with contact paper work very well.

4. Crayon pieces may be melted in muffin trays in a warm oven. These pieces, when cooled, are nice for rubbings or drawings. Crayola® makes a unit that is designed specifically for melting crayons safely.

5. Printing with tempera is easier if the tray is lined with a sponge or a paper towel.

6. A card file for art activities helps organize the program.

7. *Clay containers*. Airtight coffee cans and plastic food containers are excellent ways to keep clay moist and always ready for use.

8. *Paper scrap boxes*. By keeping two or more boxes of different sized scrap paper, children will be able to choose the paper size they want more easily.

9. Cover a wall area with pegboard and suspend heavy shopping bags or transparent plastic bags from hooks inserted in the pegboard to hold miscellaneous art supplies. Hang smocks in the same way on the pegboard (at child level, of course).

10. Use the back of a piano or bookcase to hang a shoe bag. Its pockets can hold many small items.

11. Use divided frozen food trays or a revolving lazy Susan to hold miscellaneous small items.

(From Mayesky, Mary. *Creative Activites for Young Children*, 7th ed., Clifton Park, NY: Delmar Learning.)

Be creative when thinking about storing and making materials available for your little printing masters. Storing supplies in handy boxes and other containers makes creating art and cleaning up afterward more fun.

Identifying Print-Making Materials

Materials for print making may include the following:

- *Paint*—Tempera paint in sets of eight colors, powder paint in thin mixture, food coloring, and water-soluble printing ink are all suitable.

- *Stamp pad*—Place discarded pieces of felt or cotton inside a jar lid, a cut-down milk carton, a frozen-food tin, or similar waterproof container and saturate with color.

- *Paper*—Absorbent papers that are good for printing include newsprint, manila paper, tissue, construction paper, newspaper want-ad pages, and plain wrapping paper.

- *Cloth*—Absorbent pieces of discarded cloth, such as pillow cases, torn sheets, handkerchiefs, and old T-shirts, can be printed on.

- *Other items*—Other items you might need in print making include newspaper or plastic garbage bags for covering tables, brushes for applying paint when not using stamp pads, and cans for water.

Using Food Products

Several activities in this book involve the use of different kinds of foods. There are long-standing arguments for and against food use in art activities. For example, many teachers have long used potato printing as a traditional printing activity for young children. These teachers feel potatoes are an economical way to prepare printing objects for children. Using potatoes beyond their "shelf life" is an alternative to throwing them away. On the other hand, many teachers feel that food is for eating and should be used for nothing else.

This book has many activities that do not use food so that there will be options for teachers who oppose food use in art activities. Also, where possible, alternatives to food items are suggested. Whatever your opinion, creative activities in printing are provided for your and the children's exploration and enjoyment.

Employing Safe Materials

For all the activities in this book and for any art activities for young children, be sure to use safe art supplies. Read labels on all art materials. Check for age appropriateness. The Art and Creative Materials Institute (ACMI) labels art materials AP (approved product) and CL (certified label). Products with these labels are certified safe for use by young children. The ACMI provides an extensive list of materials and manufacturers of safe materials for all young children. This information is available on the ACMI Web site at http://www.acminet.org or by writing to 715 Boylston Street, Boston, MA 02116.

Some basic safety hints for art activities are:

- Always use products that are appropriate for the child. Use nontoxic materials for children in grade six and lower.

- Never use products for skin painting or food preparation unless the products are indicated for those uses.

- Do not transfer art materials to other containers. You will lose the valuable safety information on the product package.

- Do not eat or drink while using art and craft materials. Wash after use. Clean yourself and your supplies.
- Be sure that your work area is well ventilated.

Potentially unsafe art supplies for print making include:

- *Powdered clay.* Powered clay is easily inhaled and contains silica, which harms the lungs. Instead, use wet clay, which cannot be inhaled.
- *Instant papier-mâché.* Instant papier-mâché may contain lead or asbestos. Use only black-and-white newspaper and wheat paste or liquid starch.
- *Epoxy, instant glues, or other solvent-based glues.* Use only water-based, white glue, or glue sticks.
- *Paints that require solvents like turpentine to clean.* Use only water-based paints.
- *Cold water or commercial dyes that contain chemical additives.* Use only natural vegetable dyes made from beets, onion skins, and so on.
- *Permanent markers.* Permanent markers may contain toxic solvents. Use only water-based markers.

Be aware of all children's allergies. Children with allergies to wheat, for example, may be irritated by the wheat paste used in papier-mâché. Children who are allergic to peanuts must taste nothing containing peanut butter. In fact, some centers make it a rule to avoid all peanut butter use in food and art activities. Other art materials that may cause allergic reactions include chalk or other dusty substances, water-based clay, and any material containing petroleum products.

Also be aware of children's habits. Some young children put everything in their mouths. (This can be the case at any age.) Others may be shy and slow to accept new materials. Use your knowledge of children's tendencies to help you plan art activities that are safe for all children.

Finally, take the time to talk with the children about which things they may taste and which they may not. For example, when making anything mixed with glue, remind the children that glue is not to be tasted. You may find it helpful to use a large cut-out of a smiley face with a protruding tongue to indicate an activity that is an "edible" one—one with materials the children can taste. Use a smiley face with a large black "X" over the tongue to indicate a "no-taste" activity.

Creating a Child-Friendly Environment

It is difficult to be creative when you have to worry about keeping yourself and your work area clean. Cover all work areas with newspaper. It is best to tape the newspaper to the surface to prevent paint and other materials from seeping through the spaces. In addition, it is much easier to pick up and throw away paint-spattered newspaper than to clean a tabletop. Other coverups that work well are shower curtains and plastic tablecloths.

Also remember to cover the children. Some good child coverups are men's shirts (with the sleeves cut off), aprons, pillowcases with holes cut for heads and arms, and smocks. Some fun alternatives are sets of old clothes or shoes that can be worn as "art clothes." These old clothes could become "art journals" as they become covered with the traces of various art projects.

Other things to have on hand are paper towels or scrap paper for blotting printing items when changing colors during printing. A bucket of moist, child-sized sponges are also handy for cleanup.

Creating a Child's Art Environment

Encourage young artists by displaying art prints and other works of art. Do not make the mistake of thinking young children do not enjoy "grown-up art." Children are never too young to enjoy the colors, lines, patterns, and designs of artists' work. Art posters from a local museum, for example, can brighten an art area. Such posters also get children looking at and talking about art, which encourages the children's creative work.

Display pieces of pottery, shells and rocks, and other beautiful objects from nature to encourage children's appreciation of the lines, symmetries, and colors of nature, all part of the print-making experience. Even the youngest child can enjoy the look and feel of smooth, colored rocks or the colors of fall leaves. All these are natural parts of a child's world that can be talked about with young children as those children create artwork. Beautiful objects encourage creativity.

Starting to Collect

The more exciting "extras" you can collect, the more fun the print-making activities in this book will be for the children. You cannot start too soon collecting materials for these activities. You can probably add items to the following list, which suggests some print-making materials. Ask friends and parents to start collecting some of these materials.

Paper for printing (e.g., newsprint, manila paper, wallpaper, tissue, construction paper, newspaper want ads, plain wrapping paper)

Cloth (e.g., old pillowcases, torn sheets, handkerchiefs, old T-shirts)

Spools

Buttons

Rocks

Stamp pads with washable ink

Paint, paintbrushes

"Found" objects (e.g., forks, kitchen utensils, bottle tops, sticks, corks)

Natural objects (e.g., leaves, weeds, stones, grasses)

Vegetables (e.g., potatoes, carrots, other firm vegetables)

Styrofoam trays (but not those used for meat, as they may contain salmonella)

Styrofoam or paper cups (in states where Styrofoam cups are not prohibited in licensed child-care centers)

Paper plates

Boxes of varied sizes

Pieces of screen

Enter the world of print making in the pages that follow. Enjoy the trip!

All Ages

ABCs and 123s

MATERIALS

- ☐ collection of plastic alphabet letters and numbers
- ☐ paper
- ☐ tempera paint
- ☐ shallow container for paint or stamp pad (see the "Printing Stamps" activity for more information)
- ☐ paintbrushes (optional)

💡 HELPFUL HINT

- Very young artists will enjoy this activity. They need not identify letters or numbers by name; they just enjoy printing with them. You may give the name or the letter or number as the children print. Do not overdo this, because printing is the object of the activity.

DEVELOPMENTAL GOALS

Develop creativity, small motor development, and hand-eye coordination; recognize letters and numbers; and learn the design concept of pattern.

PREPARATION

For children learning about numbers and letters, discuss the letters and their sounds. Let children who can identify the letters do so. Talk about the plastic numbers. Let children who can identify the numbers do so. Talk about how the children could make designs with letters and numbers. With toddlers, simply identify the letters and numbers.

PROCESS

1. Dip plastic alphabet letters and numbers in paint.
2. Print them on paper.
3. Encourage the children to make patterns with single letters or numbers.
4. Make more patterns or lines with other letters or numbers.
5. Let children who can print their names and ages do so.

VARIATIONS

- Print initials on several sheets of paper to make personalized, original stationery.
- Print a letter. Then, using crayons or markers, draw pictures of words that start with that letter.
- Print letters or numbers on a page leaving large spaces between each. Trace around the drawings several times with crayons or markers to make another kind of design.

NOTES FOR NEXT TIME: _____

_____

Copyright © 2004, Delmar Learning

A

All Ages

Apple Prints

MATERIALS

- ☐ apples
- ☐ tempera paint
- ☐ paper plate
- ☐ shallow tray, or wide paint brushes
- ☐ paper
- ☐ knife

💡 HELPFUL HINTS

- To paint on a T-shirt, put a thick layer of paper inside the shirt to prevent the paint from bleeding through to the back of the fabric.
- An adult must cut the apples.

DEVELOPMENTAL GOALS

Develop creativity, small motor development, and hand-eye coordination and learn the design concept of pattern.

PREPARATION

An adult must cut the apple in half through the middle or cut it from top to bottom. Middle cuts make circle stamps with stars in the middle. Top-to-bottom cuts make apple shapes.

PROCESS

1. Dip the apple in paint.
2. Press the apple onto the paper to make a print.
3. Continue printing until desired design or pattern is created.

VARIATIONS

- Decorate a T-shirt with apple designs. Be sure to get fabric paints, and be sure the children are dressed in painting smocks or old clothes.
- Brush paint onto the children's hands, and decorate a T-shirt with these special handprints.
- Use several colors of paint for printing with apples.

NOTES FOR NEXT TIME: _____

_____

_____

_____

_____

Copyright © 2004, Delmar Learning

Years Old and UP

Background Paper Experiments

MATERIALS

- [ ] first, read the following "Process" section to gather the appropriate paper
- [ ] tempera paint, and objects to print

 **HELPFUL HINTS**

- Encourage the children to find new backgrounds for prints of their own.
- Ask parents and friends to save interesting kinds of paper and other objects for printing.

DEVELOPMENTAL GOALS

To develop creativity, small motor development, and hand-eye coordination and learn the design concept of contrast.

PREPARATION

Talk with children about contrast—how light colors look against dark colors. Discuss how large things look against smaller ones. Let the children give their own examples of contrast.

PROCESS

1. Paint the background paper and allow it to dry before printing on it with contrasting color paint.
2. Paste pieces of tissue or colored construction paper onto background paper. Allow them to dry. Then, print on this paper.
3. Print a design on background paper with pieces of sponge. Allow it to dry. Then, print on this paper.
4. Draw a design with crayons or markers on a piece of paper. Print over the design.
5. Try using a variety of shapes and sizes of paper to print on.
6. Place flat objects under the paper, then rub over with the side of the crayon to reveal the pattern. Print over this pattern with thin tempera paint.

VARIATIONS

- Print on various types of cloth, such as muslin, cotton, and denim.
- Print on wood scraps.
- Print with permanent ink on old T-shirts.
- Print on pieces cut from white gift boxes. Cover with clear contact paper and use as placemats.

NOTES FOR NEXT TIME: _____

_____

_____

Berry Nice Prints

MATERIALS

- ☐ plastic berry baskets
- ☐ construction paper
- ☐ tempera paint
- ☐ container for paint (large enough to dip berry basket in)
- ☐ paper

**HELPFUL HINT**

- This is a good activity for beginning printers. The berry basket is easy to hold and to print on paper.

DEVELOPMENTAL GOALS

Develop creativity, small motor development, and hand-eye coordination and learn the design concept of line.

PREPARATION

Talk about the lines they see in the plastic berry basket. Discuss how the lines cross and how they make squares. Talk about which kind of prints the children think the baskets will make on paper.

PROCESS

1. Dip the berry basket in paint.
2. Press the basket onto the paper.
3. Repeat, overlapping shapes.
4. Continue until the pattern or design is completed.

VARIATIONS

- Make contrasting designs by printing with white paint on black paper.
- Spread glue in spots and sprinkle glitter on them for a glittery effect.
- Print with different colors of primary colors. Watch the colors mix!

NOTES FOR NEXT TIME: _____

_____

_____

_____

Copyright © 2004, Delmar Learning

Bubble Prints

MATERIALS

- ☐ 1 cup water
- ☐ food coloring
- ☐ 1/4 cup liquid detergent
- ☐ 1/4 cup liquid starch
- ☐ straws
- ☐ printing paper
- ☐ measuring cups
- ☐ 6 to 8 inch bowl

💡 HELPFUL HINTS

- Be sure children do not sip with the straws. To avoid this, poke a hole in the top of the straw.
- If the bubbles pop too quickly, add a few table-spoons of sugar to the water.

DEVELOPMENTAL GOALS

Develop creativity, small motor development, and hand-eye coordination and use familiar materials in new ways.

PREPARATION

In a 6 to 8 inch bowl, mix the water, drops of food coloring, liquid detergent, and liquid starch. Let the children do the measuring and mixing.

PROCESS

1. Blow bubbles using a straw.
2. Blow until the bubbles form a structure above the rim of the bowl.
3. Make a print by laying a sheet of white paper across the bowl rim and allowing the bubbles to pop against the paper.
4. Talk about the lines, shapes, and patterns the bubbles make on the paper.

VARIATIONS

- Use newspaper or brown wrapping paper.
- Use the printed paper for stationery or gift wrap.
- Have two or three bowls of differently colored bubble mixture. Make bubble prints with all the colors. Talk about how the colors mix.
- Make bubble prints outside on a sunny day.
- Blow bubbles with paper towel tubes.

NOTES FOR NEXT TIME: _____

_____

Copyright © 2004, Delmar Learning

PRINT MAKING 5

All Ages

Can-Top Prints

MATERIALS

- ☐ all sizes of cans (e.g., juice, spray-can tops, bottle caps, soup cans)
- ☐ paper
- ☐ paint in shallow containers

 **HELPFUL HINTS**

- This is a good beginning printing activity because it concentrates on one shape and allows the children to concentrate on the process.
- Young printers are easily distracted by too many materials.
- Give children large sheets of paper for this activity, particularly if it is the children's first time. Let them experiment with making designs of their choosing.
- Later, give a group of children a large piece of butcher paper that covers part of a bulletin board and let the little printers print to their hearts' content.
- Give other groups the paper that will complete a bulletin-board cover. Cover your bulletin board with this paper as a background for your displays.

DEVELOPMENTAL GOALS

Develop creativity, small motor development, and hand-eye coordination; use familiar objects in new ways; learn the design concept of pattern and use a circle and its variations to make a pattern.

PREPARATION

Talk about the circular shape and the sizes of the cans. Discuss the idea of pattern—repeating a design on the paper. Wash the cans thoroughly and let them dry.

PROCESS

1. Give each child a piece of paper.
2. Dip the can lightly in paint.
3. Make a print on the paper with the can top.
4. Make can top prints in vertical lines, circular lines, zigzags, and so on.
5. See how many different kinds of designs the children can make with the can top.

VARIATIONS

- Add other circular objects, like paper-towel and tissue rolls, to the print.
- Provide small boxes of rectangular or square shapes to use for printing another shape.
- Use different kinds of paper, like newsprint, classified ads, brown wrapping paper.

NOTES FOR NEXT TIME: _____

_____

_____

PRINT MAKING

Copyright © 2004, Delmar Learning

Cardboard or Rubber Block Prints

MATERIALS

- ☐ a piece of innertube or cardboard
- ☐ scissors
- ☐ paste or glue
- ☐ heavy cardboard
- ☐ floor tile or a piece of wood
- ☐ thick mixture of tempera paint
- ☐ spoon
- ☐ brayer (or small trim paint roller)
- ☐ ink slab (9" × 9" floor tile or piece of Plexiglas®/clear plastic with edges taped)
- ☐ paper
- ☐ newspaper

💡 HELPFUL HINTS

- This is an excellent activity for experienced print makers, children generally 5 years and older.

- Use scrap paper for practice prints to get the children used to using a brayer or roller.

- Use a smooth bottom of a small jar to rub the entire design before printing.

- Peel back a corner of the paper to see whether further rubbing is necessary for a strong print.

DEVELOPMENTAL GOALS

Develop creativity, small motor development, and hand-eye coordination; practice using a brayer; and learn the design concepts of shape, line, and pattern.

PREPARATION

Discuss which designs the children would like to make and print. Talk about how to make a pattern by repeating designs or objects. Give the children time to practice using a brayer (roller) if the children have never used a brayer before.

PROCESS

1. Cut shapes from pieces of cardboard or inner tubes and glue them to a cardboard background for printing.

2. Spoon a small amount of paint onto the piece of Plexiglas® or floor tile.

3. Roll the ink with a brayer (or small trim paint roller) until it is spread smoothly on the inking slab.

4. Roll the ink brayer over the mounted design from side and top to bottom to ensure an even distribution over the entire surface.

5. Place a piece of paper over the inked design and rub gently and evenly with the fingers until the entire design is reproduced.

6. Re-ink the design for more prints.

VARIATIONS

- Use water-soluble or oil base printer's ink. This produces a very clear print. If you use oil-base printer's ink, you will need to use turpentine to clean the brayer.

- Try different shapes, sizes, and colors of paper for printing.

- Print on fabric squares. Join all the different prints for a group "print quilt."

NOTES FOR NEXT TIME: _____

_____

Copyright © 2004, Delmar Learning

Cardboard Relief Prints

MATERIALS

☐ pieces of cardboard

☐ carpenter's nails

☐ thick tempera paint

☐ paper

☐ paintbrushes

💡 HELPFUL HINTS

• Use small paint rollers to roll out the paint onto the cardboard.

• Use nails long and big enough for children to handle like pencils. A ten-penny nail works well.

NOTES FOR NEXT TIME:

_____

_____

_____

_____

_____

DEVELOPMENTAL GOALS

Develop creativity, small motor development, and hand-eye coordination; learn the design concepts of pattern and line; and understand relief printing.

PREPARATION

Discuss what relief printing is—printing from a raised surface. A simple example of relief printing is a rubber stamp pressed into a stamp pad and pressed onto a piece of paper. Relief printing plates are made from flat sheets of material (in this activity—cardboard). After drawing a picture on the surface, the artist uses tools to cut away the areas that will not be printed.

PROCESS

1. Scratch out a design on the cardboard with a carpenter's nail.

2. Remember that the printed image will appear in reverse!

3. Use a paintbrush to cover the cardboard with tempera paint.

4. Lay the paper on top.

5. Press lightly with the palm of the hand.

6. Peel away the paper and see the print!

VARIATIONS

• Instead of drawing into the Styrofoam, press areas you do not want printed.

• You could also cut out sections of the Styrofoam, ink them up separately, pop the pieces back together, and print.

• Repeat the process so you have an edition of prints.

• Use different colors, shapes and kinds of paper to make relief prints.

Copyright © 2004, Delmar Learning

Circle Challenge

MATERIALS

- ☐ paper cups of various sizes
- ☐ large, round pasta, and any other circular shapes to print
- ☐ tempera paint
- ☐ shallow container for paint
- ☐ brushes
- ☐ paper

💡 HELPFUL HINT

- This is a good beginning printing activity for very young artists. Only one or two circular objects are required for very young artists. This is because they are learning the process, and too many choices for printing objects distracts them. As children grow more adept in the process, add more objects for printing.

DEVELOPMENTAL GOALS

Develop creativity, small motor development, and hand-eye coordination and recognize shapes.

PREPARATION

Talk about circles. Have the children identify as many circles as they can in the room. Discuss which circular things the children can think of to use in print making. Challenge the children to bring from home as many of these items as they can. Include these items with those listed previously.

PROCESS

1. Begin by printing with one circular printing object.
2. Print this on the page, making a pattern or a random design.
3. Use another circular object and print with it on the page.
4. Try printing one line with one size circle.
5. Do another with a differently sized circle.
6. Alternate large and small circular shapes in one line.
7. Print zigzag, horizontal, and vertical lines with circle shapes.

VARIATIONS

- Repeat the activity with another shape—square, rectangle, even triangles!
- Have several containers of different colors of paint. Print each shape with a different color.
- Let the print dry. Then, print more circular shapes over the existing print using black or white tempera paint for a contrasting effect.

NOTES FOR NEXT TIME: _____

_____

Cloth Prints

MATERIALS

- ☐ soft cloth
- ☐ felt markers (permanent markers if cloth is going to be washed and water-soluble markers if cloth is not going to be washed)
- ☐ heavy paper (recycled gift boxes work well)
- ☐ practice paper

💡 HELPFUL HINTS

- When using permanent markers for this activity, be sure the children are well covered so they get no marker on their clothing.
- Embroidery hoops help hold the fabric taut when the printing is done.

DEVELOPMENTAL GOALS

Develop creativity, small motor development, hand-eye coordination; learn the design concepts of pattern and line; and use familiar materials in new ways.

PREPARATION

Discuss pattern—how it is made of a repeating figure or design. Talk about how shapes can be used to make a pattern.

PROCESS

1. Cut shapes from heavy paper. Recycled gift boxes work well.
2. Trace around the shapes on the practice paper.
3. Repeat the shapes until a pattern emerges.
4. Encourage the children to do such things as overlap, turn, and reverse shapes.
5. Once the practice design on paper is made, repeat it on cloth.
6. Each child helps another by holding the paper shape in place as the other traces around it.
7. Complete the practice design on the cloth.

VARIATIONS

- Cut seasonal shapes, such as leaves in the fall, and make a design on cloth with them.
- Use "found" objects to print on the cloth, such as bottle caps, and buttons.

NOTES FOR NEXT TIME: _____

_____

_____

_____

Copyright © 2004, Delmar Learning

Cork Prints

3 Years Old and Up

MATERIALS

- ☐ corks
- ☐ knife
- ☐ paper
- ☐ paint
- ☐ paintbrushes
- ☐ newspapers
- ☐ scrap paper or paper towels (for practicing)

HELPFUL HINT

- Cut the corks before introducing the activity.

NOTES FOR NEXT TIME:

_____

_____

_____

_____

_____

DEVELOPMENTAL GOALS

Develop creativity, small motor development, and hand-eye coordination; use familiar objects in new ways; learn the design concepts of pattern and circle.

PREPARATION

Cut a design around the edge and/or in the middle of the corks.

PROCESS

1. Place a pad of newspapers under the paper to be printed.
2. Have a scrap paper or paper towel available to practice the design.
3. Cover the surface of the cork with paint.
4. Print on a scrap of paper to eliminate any excess paint.
5. Press the cork onto the paper to make a print.
6. Continue making prints to make a design or a pattern.

VARIATIONS

- Use several different colors of paint.
- Try different paper, such as brown wrapping paper, classified ads, or tissue paper.
- Apply different colors to different areas of the cork for interesting print results.

Copyright © 2004, Delmar Learning

Crayon Prints

MATERIALS

- ☐ wax crayon
- ☐ copy paper
- ☐ turpentine or mineral spirits
- ☐ shallow container
- ☐ brush
- ☐ cloth or paper towel

HELPFUL HINTS

- Mineral spirits is a solvent similar to turpentine. It is available in hardware or art-supply stores.

- Be careful that children do not get mineral spirits in their eyes. If they do, rinse the eyes thoroughly with water.

- This activity is inappropriate for beginning printers, because it involves waiting until the wax softens and the use of mineral spirits. It is appropriate for children ages 5 and up.

DEVELOPMENTAL GOALS

Develop creativity, small motor development, and hand-eye coordination and use familiar tools (crayons) in new ways.

PREPARATION

Discuss which type of picture or design the children will want to make.

PROCESS

1. Give each child a piece of copy paper.
2. Draw heavily with the crayon on the piece of paper.
3. The adult dips the brush in the mineral spirits and spreads a thin coat of mineral spirits on the back to soften the crayon wax.
4. When the wax is soft, lay a piece of paper over the picture and rub it with fingers or a flat tool until the picture transfers.
5. It may be possible to make several prints from one drawing.

VARIATIONS

- Make the crayon drawing over a piece of window screen for an interesting effect.
- Use different sizes, shapes, and kinds of paper for printing.

NOTES FOR NEXT TIME: _____

_____

Copyright © 2004, Delmar Learning

Crayon Shavings Prints

MATERIALS

- ☐ scrap pieces of crayon
- ☐ scraping tool (e.g., nail file, scissors, grater)
- ☐ aluminum foil
- ☐ paper
- ☐ salt shaker
- ☐ iron
- ☐ newspapers

💡 HELPFUL HINTS

- Exercise extreme caution around the children during the ironing processes in this activity. Only an adult should handle the iron and well away from the children's reach.
- This activity is appropriate for children who have printing experience.
- Give the children several chances to create a crayon-shavings print. As the children work with crayon shavings, they will learn how many to shake onto the paper to get a vibrant print.

DEVELOPMENTAL GOALS

Develop creativity, small motor development, and hand-eye coordination and use familiar tools (old crayons) in new ways.

PREPARATION

Have the children help shave scrap crayon into small pieces onto a piece of newspaper. Place the pieces in a clean, dry salt shaker or use any type of shaker with fairly large holes.

PROCESS

1. Sprinkle a few of the crayon shavings onto a piece of white paper.
2. Place this paper on a piece of newspaper.
3. Place a piece of foil over the crayon pieces.
4. An adult presses the foil with a moderately hot iron.
5. Remove the foil and place it on a second sheet of paper.
6. Press once again.
7. Separate the foil from the white paper, which has received the printed impression.

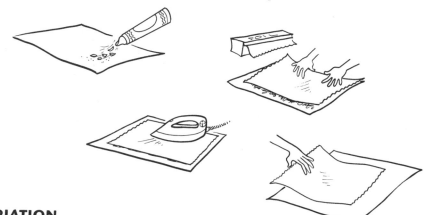

VARIATION

- To control color areas, fill several shakers with different colors of crayon shavings.

NOTES FOR NEXT TIME: _____

_____

Creative Shoe Prints

MATERIALS

- ☐ white canvas tennis shoes
- ☐ tempera paint
- ☐ printing objects such as vegetables
- ☐ plastic letters and numbers
- ☐ cotton swabs
- ☐ paintbrushes
- ☐ stamp pad (see the "Printing Stamps" activity on page 33)
- ☐ fabric crayons and pens (optional)

💡 HELPFUL HINTS

- Even very young artists ages 2 and up can decorate their own shoes.
- There may be some running of colors if the shoes get too wet. This is not a problem if you use printer's ink or fabric crayons.

DEVELOPMENTAL GOALS

Develop creativity, small motor development, and hand-eye coordination and use art to decorate everyday objects.

PREPARATION

Each child needs a pair of white tennis shoes to decorate. Talk with the children about how they would like to decorate their shoes. Talk about shapes, patterns, and designs. Discuss types of lines, too.

PROCESS

1. Dip a printing object into tempera paint.
2. Press the object onto the shoe.
3. Repeat printing with the object and others.
4. Use paintbrushes and cotton swabs to make more designs on the shoes.
5. Dip plastic letters and numbers in paint.
6. Press them onto the shoes to print.
7. Let the shoes dry thoroughly before wearing.

VARIATIONS

- Paint the shoelaces, too. Take them out and lay them on some paper and start painting!
- Use school colors and have a pair of shoes that show school spirit. Alternately, use the colors of a favorite team.
- Fabric pens and crayons work great for drawing designs on the shoes.

NOTES FOR NEXT TIME: _____

_____

Copyright © 2004, Delmar Learning

Dip It!

MATERIALS

- ☐ two or three colors of thin tempera paint of bright colors
- ☐ shallow containers
- ☐ white paper napkins or white paper towels

💡 HELPFUL HINTS

- Young children may need help folding the napkins or paper towels.
- These "tie-dyed" napkins can be used for various things, such as borders for bulletin boards or pictures, basket linings, and wrapping paper.

DEVELOPMENTAL GOALS

Develop creativity, small motor development, and hand-eye coordination; use familiar objects in new ways; and learn the design concept of pattern.

PREPARATION

Put the paint in small containers, about 1 to 1-1/2 inches deep.

PROCESS

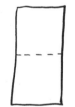

1. Give each child a white napkin or a sheet torn from a roll of white paper towels.
2. Fold the sheet in half twice.
3. Dip the corners of the napkin or towel into different colors of paint.
4. Open the napkins or towels and allow them to dry.
5. The sheets dry into multicolored, bright designs.

VARIATIONS

- Dip the same corner into two different colors. Watch the colors blend.
- Refold the dried napkin and redip it into different colors.
- Use square pieces of muslin instead of paper napkins.

NOTES FOR NEXT TIME: _____

_____

_____

_____

Finger Paint Prints

MATERIALS

- ☐ finger paint
- ☐ formica tabletop, enamel-topped table, or linoleum
- ☐ newsprint paper

💡 HELPFUL HINTS

- This is a good way to save on the cost of finger paint paper and to try something new and fun.

- Some children may finish this activity quickly. Have enough newsprint paper available so they can make several finger paint prints.

- Be careful so that you do not rub too hard when transferring the finger painting to the newsprint. It may smear the painting. If this happens, just finger paint again and lay another piece of newsprint over it. The children get to finger paint again, which is just more fun!

DEVELOPMENTAL GOALS

Develop creativity, small motor development, and hand-eye coordination and gain initial experience with printing.

PREPARATION

Mix finger paints to a thick consistency.

PROCESS

1. Put a blob of finger paint directly on the tabletop.
2. Have the child finger paint directly on the tabletop.
3. When the child is finished painting, lay a piece of newsprint paper on the finger painting.
4. Gently rub the paper with one hand.
5. The finger paint transfers from the tabletop to the paper.

VARIATIONS

- Use several colors of finger paint and watch the colors mix.
- For children who do not like to use their fingers, let them brush the finger paint around on the tabletop.

NOTES FOR NEXT TIME: _____

_____

_____

Copyright © 2004, Delmar Learning

A

All Ages

Finger Prints

MATERIALS

- ☐ stamp pad filled with washable ink or shallow container of paint
- ☐ paper
- ☐ markers
- ☐ crayons

HELPFUL HINTS

- Some children may not want to put their fingers in the paint. Do not force them to do so. Have other items these children can use to print.

- After this activity has been introduced, you will probably see these prints every time the children get around paint!

- This is a good printing activity for young children because the prints are easily done, are relatively error proof, and unique.

DEVELOPMENTAL GOALS

Develop creativity, small motor development, and hand-eye coordination and learn the design concepts of pattern, line, and swirl.

PREPARATION

Have the children practice making their finger prints. Talk about how each child's finger prints are unique. Talk about the lines the children see: swirls, curvy, round. Discuss which designs or objects the children could make with their finger prints.

PROCESS

1. Give each child a piece of paper and a stamp pad. (See the "Printing Stamps" activity on page 33 to learn how to make simple stamp pads.)

2. Show the children how to place the ball of the finger in the paint and then make a print on paper.

3. Let the children practice to learn just how much paint is necessary and the best technique for making clear prints.

4. On a clean sheet of paper, make about six prints.

5. Put each child's name on the paper and let the paper dry.

6. Make characters or objects using the finger prints as the body.

VARIATIONS

- Make a picture using finger prints.

- Make a finger-print family. Draw the family members in their house or outside in the sun.

- Use different colors of paint, different kinds of paper.

NOTES FOR NEXT TIME: _____

_____

_____

_____

First Experiments with Monoprints

MATERIALS

- ☐ thick mixture of tempera paint
- ☐ paintbrushes
- ☐ sheets of Plexiglas® (approximately 12" × 12")
- ☐ paper
- ☐ small paint roller (optional)
- ☐ Popsicle stick or pencil with eraser

💡 HELPFUL HINTS

- You can find Plexiglas® at a local lumberyard or hardware store. Ask for offcuts, which are normally thrown away.

- You can also use old political-yard signs, garage-sale signs, or any waxy-surface signs for the printing plate.

- Add flour to tempera paint to make it thicker and stickier like printer's ink.

DEVELOPMENTAL GOALS

Develop creativity, small motor development, and hand-eye coordination and learn the concept of monoprinting.

PREPARATION

Explain that monoprinting is the process of making only one print from the printing plate (the part on which the picture is first drawn).

PROCESS

1. Brush the paint onto the Plexiglas®, covering it completely, or use a small paint roller to roll it out to cover the Plexiglas®.

2. Using the end of a pencil or a Popsicle stick, draw an image on the Plexiglas®.

3. Place the paper on the Plexiglas® and rub lightly.

4. Peel away the paper and see the print.

VARIATIONS

- Repeat the process using a different color of paint and a different kind of paper.

- Use found objects to make a design on the paint. Make a monoprint of this design.

NOTES FOR NEXT TIME: _____

_____

_____

Copyright © 2004, Delmar Learning

Glue and Leaf Prints

MATERIALS

- ☐ white glue
- ☐ leaves
- ☐ pieces of cardboard
- ☐ paint
- ☐ paintbrushes
- ☐ paper to print on

💡 HELPFUL HINTS

- Beginning printers often enjoy printing without creating patterns or designs. Expect random printing when children learn new art techniques.

- Both fallen leaves and green leaves work for this activity.

DEVELOPMENTAL GOALS

Develop creativity, small motor development, and hand-eye coordination and learn the design concepts of pattern and line.

PREPARATION

Collect leaves of different sizes and shapes. Talk about the leaves and their shapes and sizes. Discuss how the children can use the leaves to make patterns. Cut cardboard into pieces that are slightly bigger than the leaves.

PROCESS

1. Squeeze white glue around edges of the top side of a leaf.
2. Stick the leaf to a piece of cardboard.
3. Use a paintbrush to cover the leaf with paint.
4. Press the painted side of the leaf onto a piece of paper.
5. Repeat to make a design.

VARIATIONS

- Include sticks, pine cones, and other natural objects. Dip them into paint and add them to the leaf design.
- Use different colors of paint.
- Use different kinds of paper, such as tissue, classified ads, brown wrapping paper.

NOTES FOR NEXT TIME: _____

_____

_____

_____

Great Balls of Fun!

MATERIALS

- ☐ paper
- ☐ thin mixture of tempera paint
- ☐ containers for paint
- ☐ tennis balls
- ☐ smocks or old clothes for covering the children

💡 HELPFUL HINTS

- This is a great outdoor activity because the mess is not a worry.
- Some dripping may occur, which adds interest to the finished print.

DEVELOPMENTAL GOALS

Develop creativity, small motor development, and hand-eye coordination and use familiar objects in new ways.

PREPARATION

Be sure children and the area are well covered. This is a very messy, but fun activity!

PROCESS

1. Dip the tennis ball in paint.
2. Dab or drop the balls onto the paper to make a print.
3. Repeat until satisfied with the print.
4. Let the prints dry thoroughly.

VARIATIONS

- Use balls of different sizes and weights. Golf balls leave interesting prints.
- Dip balls in different colors.
- Print on a piece of cloth or an old T-shirt using printer's ink for a permanent print.

NOTES FOR NEXT TIME: _____

_____

_____

_____

Copyright © 2004, Delmar Learning

A

All Ages

Hair's the Thing

MATERIALS

- ☐ old combs
- ☐ brushes (e.g., hairbrushes, scrub brushes, toothbrushes)
- ☐ paper
- ☐ tempera paint
- ☐ shallow container for paint or stamp pad (see the "Printing Stamps" activity for directions.)

💡 HELPFUL HINTS

- With very young artists, use only one or two combs or brushes. Because these children are learning the process, too many items may confuse them.

- Run the combs and brushes through the dishwasher or soak them in soapy water before using them for this activity.

DEVELOPMENTAL GOALS

Develop creativity, small motor development, and hand-eye coordination and use familiar objects in new ways.

PREPARATION

Have children bring in brushes and combs that they can use for printing. Be sure the children know the brushes and combs must be old, because paint will not come out of them after printing.

PROCESS

1. Dip the comb into tempera paint.
2. Run the comb along the paper to make wavy printed lines.
3. Dip the comb in paint again and find another way to make marks with it.
4. Dip a brush into the paint.
5. Press the brush, dab it, and rub it along the paper to make more prints.
6. Use another brush and repeat the process.

VARIATIONS

- Have several colors of paint. Use a different one with each brush or comb.
- Paint the items with a paintbrush, then press them onto the paper.
- Print using as many sides of the combs/brushes as possible.

NOTES FOR NEXT TIME: _____

_____

_____

_____

Copyright © 2004, Delmar Learning

Hand and Foot Prints

MATERIALS

- ☐ long piece of paper
- ☐ tempera paint in a shallow pan large enough to put feet and hands in
- ☐ pail of water with a bit of liquid detergent mixed in
- ☐ paper towels
- ☐ tape

💡 HELPFUL HINTS

- This is a great outdoor activity! Children will enjoy being outside and playing barefoot.

- Some children may not want to put their feet or hands in paint. Trace around their feet and hands with a marker or crayon.

DEVELOPMENTAL GOALS

To develop creativity, small motor development, and hand-eye coordination and develop an initial understanding of how prints are made.

PREPARATION

This is a fun but messy activity. Spread newspapers and tape them to the floor. Spread out the long piece of paper and tape it to the newspaper.

PROCESS

1. Have the children dip their feet in the paint.
2. Print the right foot and left foot.
3. Print the hands.
4. Write the child's name by the prints.
5. Continue until all children have made their prints.
6. Step into the pail of water to clean off the feet. Dip in the hands to clean them, too. Dry with paper towels.

VARIATIONS

- After making the first set of prints, let the child walk to the end of the paper, making a trail of footprints until the paint is "walked off."
- Use the foot and hand print sheet as a bulletin board for an "All About Us" theme.
- Print foot and hand prints on separate pieces of paper. Write down what the children want to tell about themselves near the prints. This could be the cover of a book "All About Me."

NOTES FOR NEXT TIME: _____

_____

_____

_____

Copyright © 2004, Delmar Learning

A

All Ages

Kitchen Prints

MATERIALS

- ☐ kitchen utensils and equipment to be used for printing
- ☐ tempera paint
- ☐ shallow container for paint
- ☐ paper

 **HELPFUL HINT**

- This is a good activity to help develop children's thinking skills. It helps the children see things in the environment for their potential as art materials.

NOTES FOR NEXT TIME:

_____

_____

_____

_____

_____

DEVELOPMENTAL GOALS

Develop creativity, small motor development, and hand-eye coordination and use familiar objects in new ways.

PREPARATION

Challenge the children to come up with as many things in the kitchen that they can print (e.g., potato masher, forks, spoons, bowls, paper cups, spatula, funnels, wire strainers).

PROCESS

1. Choose one object with which to print.
2. Dip the object in tempera paint.
3. Press the object onto the paper.
4. Try printing on a different side of the same utensil.
5. Print with other utensils using various sides.
6. Try making a line with one kind of utensil.
7. Make another line using another utensil.
8. Alternate printing with different utensils for another type of pattern.

VARIATIONS

- Use several colors of paint. Use a different color for different utensils.
- Print on different shapes, colors, and kinds of paper.
- Use another room in the house for objects. For example, challenge the children to find as many objects as they can from their own bedrooms, bathrooms, or garages.

Copyright © 2004, Delmar Learning

Monoprints One More Time!

MATERIALS

- ☐ thick mixture of tempera paint
- ☐ paintbrushes
- ☐ sheets of Plexiglas® (12" × 12")
- ☐ paper
- ☐ small paint roller (optional)
- ☐ paper
- ☐ pencil

💡 HELPFUL HINTS

- Add flour to tempera to make it thicker and stickier like printer's ink.
- You can find Plexiglas® at hardware stores or lumber yards. Ask for off-cuts they often throw away.
- Old yard signs or political signs also work well. Any sturdy paper with a waxy surface works, too.

DEVELOPMENTAL GOALS

Develop creativity, small motor development, and hand-eye coordination and understand monoprinting.

PREPARATION

Discuss monoprinting—a process in which only one print is made from the printing plate (the part on which the picture/design is made).

PROCESS

1. Cover the Plexiglas® completely by brushing on the tempera paint. Or you can use a small paint roller to roll it on the Plexiglas®.
2. Place paper over the Plexiglas®.
3. Using a pencil, draw an image on the paper.
4. When you peel away the paper, the image will have transferred itself.
5. This is similar to carbon paper.

VARIATIONS

- Make a design using different thicknesses of pencils.
- Use sticks and twigs to make the design.
- Print with different kinds of paper and different colors of paint.

NOTES FOR NEXT TIME: _____

_____

_____

_____

_____

Copyright © 2004, Delmar Learning

Years Old and Up

Monoprints—Even One More Way!

MATERIALS

- ☐ tempera paint
- ☐ paintbrushes
- ☐ sheets of Plexiglas® (approximately 12" × 12")
- ☐ paper

💡 HELPFUL HINTS

- Thicken the tempera paint with a little bit of flour to make it sticky like printer's ink.
- You can find Plexiglas® at lumber yards or hardware stores. Ask for offcuts that are normally thrown away.
- Old yard signs or political signs work well, too.

DEVELOPMENTAL GOALS

Develop creativity, small motor development, and hand-eye coordination and understand monoprinting.

PREPARATION

Discuss monoprinting. Explain that it is a process of making only one print from the printing plate (the part that holds the picture/design).

PROCESS

1. Using a paintbrush, paint a design or picture on the Plexiglas®.
2. Use many or a few colors.
3. Do not let the paint dry!
4. Place paper over the Plexiglas®.
5. Rub lightly with the palm of the hand.
6. Peel the paper away.

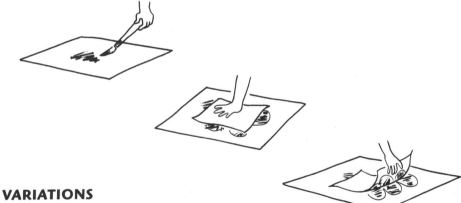

VARIATIONS

- Use small and large paintbrushes in the design. Even try a house paint type of paintbrush!
- Try different sizes and colors of paper.

NOTES FOR NEXT TIME: _____

_____

_____

_____

Nature Spatter Prints

MATERIALS

- ☐ toothbrushes
- ☐ paint
- ☐ leaves
- ☐ weeds
- ☐ grasses
- ☐ paper
- ☐ pieces of screen

💡 HELPFUL HINTS

- Spatter painting is messy but fun. Be sure to prepare the area and the children.

- Encourage the children to take time to arrange and rearrange their items until they create designs they like. Some children will do this quickly; others will need more time.

- Spatter prints are more interesting in contrasting colors or paint.

DEVELOPMENTAL GOALS

Develop creativity, small motor development, and hand-eye coordination and see design and pattern in nature.

PREPARATION

Put paint in small, shallow containers. Talk about the natural objects collected for this project. Discuss how the children could arrange the objects on the paper. Demonstrate how to rub the toothbrush across the screen and over the paper to get paint spatters on the paper.

PROCESS

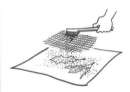

1. Arrange the natural objects on the paper in a design.
2. Dip the toothbrush in the paint.
3. Rub the paint-filled toothbrush across a piece of screen over a part of the arrangement on the paper.

4. Paint will spatter on the paper around the arrangement.
5. Continue spatter painting until the whole area around the arrangement is covered with paint spatters.
6. Remove the arrangement to see the print.

VARIATIONS

- Use different colors of paint.
- Use different kinds of paper, such as brown wrapping paper, white tissue paper, and construction paper.

NOTES FOR NEXT TIME: _____

_____

_____

_____

Copyright © 2004, Delmar Learning

5
<small>Years Old and Up</small>

Paint Monoprints

DEVELOPMENTAL GOALS

Develop creativity, small motor development, and hand-eye coordination and learn the design concept of mirror image.

MATERIALS

☐ smooth, nonabsorbent hard surface (e.g., glass, plastic, tabletop)
☐ drawing paper
☐ tempera paint
☐ brush
☐ water container

PREPARATION

Discuss which kind of pattern, design, or picture the children may want to do. Remind the children that rubbing on a painting with another piece of paper will result in a mirror image. Talk about what a mirror image is—the reverse image.

PROCESS

1. Paint a picture or design on a nonabsorbent surface.

2. Allow the surface to dry.
3. Thoroughly dampen a sheet of drawing paper.
4. Press the dampened paper firmly and evenly over the painted design with the palm of the hand.
5. Carefully peel the paper from the design.
6. One impression printing will appear on the paper as a mirror image.

(💡) HELPFUL HINT

• This is an excellent printing activity for older children, because the children are more able to wait for the painting to dry. They can also dampen the drawing paper themselves.

NOTES FOR NEXT TIME:

_____

_____

_____

VARIATION

• Older children may enjoy including names or numbers on their designs. They will have to draw them backward for them to print correctly. This is a definite challenge!

Copyright © 2004, Delmar Learning

Pasta Prints

MATERIALS

- ☐ all shapes of pasta (e.g., elbows, shells, wheels, spaghetti)
- ☐ paste
- ☐ construction paper
- ☐ tempera paint
- ☐ shallow containers for paint
- ☐ paper for printing

💡 HELPFUL HINT

- Because the pasta is bumpy, the whole piece will not print on the paper. It will still make an interesting print.

- Do not use buttons or beads with children three years and younger.

DEVELOPMENTAL GOALS

Develop creativity, small motor development, and hand-eye coordination and learn the design concepts of shapes and pattern.

PREPARATION

Discuss the various shapes of pasta. Talk about how the shapes could make designs or patterns.

PROCESS

1. Paste pasta pieces onto construction paper.
2. Make a design, picture, or pattern.
3. Brush tempera paint over the pasta design.
4. Press a piece of paper over the pasta.
5. Tap lightly over the pasta with the palm of the hand.
6. Remove the paper and see the print.

VARIATIONS

- For those who are opposed to using food in art activities, use such non-food items as buttons and beads.
- Include other items in the design, such as buttons, rice, and twigs.
- Brush again over the pasta with a different color of paint. Make another pasta print.
- Encourage the children to make patterns with the pasta. Try alternating shapes in a line. Make one line of one type of pasta, another line with a different kind.

NOTES FOR NEXT TIME: _____

_____

_____

Copyright © 2004, Delmar Learning

A

All Ages

Pine Cone Prints

MATERIALS

- ☐ pine cones
- ☐ thin mixture of tempera paint
- ☐ container for paint
- ☐ paper

 **HELPFUL HINT**

- If pine trees are not in your area, buy bags of pine cones at craft stores.

DEVELOPMENTAL GOALS

Develop creativity, small motor development, and hand-eye coordination and appreciate pattern and beauty in nature.

PREPARATION

Go outdoors and collect pine cones. Talk about their shapes, how they feel, and how they smell.

PROCESS

1. Give each child a piece of paper.
2. Dip a pine cone in tempera paint.
3. Press the pine cone onto the paper.
4. Use all sides of the pine cone to make prints.

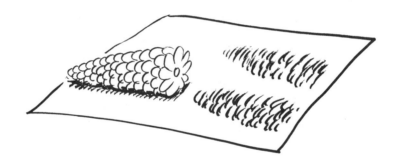

VARIATIONS

- Include twigs, acorns, and small stones for printing.
- Save painted pine cones to use as part of natural arrangements.

NOTES FOR NEXT TIME: _____

_____

_____

_____

Copyright © 2004, Delmar Learning

Play Dough Prints

MATERIALS

- ☐ play dough
- ☐ Popsicle or craft sticks
- ☐ paper
- ☐ tempera paint
- ☐ shallow containers for paint

HELPFUL HINTS

- Young children may enjoy simply printing with the play dough without carving designs. This is to be expected with beginning printers.
- Encourage speedy finishers to make several different carvings to print.

DEVELOPMENTAL GOALS

Develop creativity, small motor development, and hand-eye coordination and learn the design concept of pattern.

PREPARATION

Discuss stamps and how to print with them. Talk about which kind of stamps the children would like to make from play dough.

PROCESS

1. Give the child a lump of play dough the size of an apple or a small grapefruit.
2. Pound the play dough into small, flat cakes about 1 inch thick.
3. Carve a design on the flat surface with a Popsicle or craft stick.
4. Brush the design with paint or dip it in paint.
5. Press the design onto paper to print.

VARIATIONS

- Carve several different designs on the play dough. Print each in a different color.
- Carve letters or numbers. Print on sheets of paper to make original stationery.
- Make one line of one design, then another of a second design. Try alternating two designs in one line.
- Print horizontal, vertical, and zigzag lines.
- Printed sheets make great wrapping paper, backing for photos, and covers for jars.

NOTES FOR NEXT TIME: _____

_____

Copyright © 2004, Delmar Learning

All Ages

Plunge into It!

MATERIALS

- ☐ new plungers of various sizes
- ☐ large sheets of butcher paper
- ☐ various colors of tempera paint
- ☐ foam trays or plates

 **HELPFUL HINTS**

- This is a great outdoor activity!
- Foot and hand prints are a logical next step from this activity. They can be added to the print after the plunger prints are done.

DEVELOPMENTAL GOALS

Develop creativity, large and small motor development, and hand-eye coordination and learn the design concepts of pattern and circular shapes.

PREPARATION

Cover the art area with newspaper. Tape the newspaper to the floor. Lay out butcher paper, and tape it to the floor, as well. Prepare paints in trays. Set plungers in paint trays.

PROCESS

1. Dip the plunger in paint.
2. Press the plunger onto the butcher paper to make a print.
3. Continue printing to create a design or pattern.

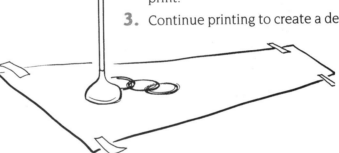

VARIATIONS

- Add other round objects to print, such as paper cups or towel rolls.
- Use two plungers at a time—each with a different color of paint.
- Use the paper as a giant class mural.
- Use the print as wrapping paper or book covers.

NOTES FOR NEXT TIME: _____

_____

_____

_____

Copyright © 2004, Delmar Learning

Print All Over—Body Part Prints

MATERIALS

- ☐ tempera paint
- ☐ large sheets of paper
- ☐ shallow pans
- ☐ old hand towels

💡 HELPFUL HINTS

- This is a great activity for outdoors! Outside, the children can rinse themselves in soapy water, hose off, and dry with old towels.

- Be prepared for prints that are a bit unusual—such as bottom prints. If you have prepared the children in old painting clothes, the unusual will not be a problem.

- This activity is appropriate for even very young artists, because it is simple and easy to do and understand.

DEVELOPMENTAL GOALS

Develop creativity, small motor development, and hand-eye coordination and explore a new print technique.

PREPARATION

If the children have done hand and foot prints, talk about the process. Discuss which other parts of the body the children can print with (e.g., nose, chin, knee, forearm).

Make a stamp pad by folding old hand towels into thirds. The towels should be about 7" × 14" with three layers. Soak each towel with tempera paint and place it in a cookie sheet or another shallow pan.

PROCESS

1. Press a body part on the pad and then on the paper.
2. Let the child make as many prints of as many body parts as desired.
3. Give child enough paper to make more if they are interested.

VARIATIONS

- Have several color stamp pads for multicolor body prints.
- Tape a long sheet of paper to the wall and print on it.
- Print on pieces of muslin.
- Use printed sheets for wrapping paper or for background on bulletin boards.

NOTES FOR NEXT TIME: _____

_____

_____

_____

Copyright © 2004, Delmar Learning

Printing Stamps

MATERIALS

- ☐ string
- ☐ glue
- ☐ block of wood
- ☐ paper
- ☐ thin mixture of tempera paint
- ☐ brush
- ☐ shallow container for paint

💡 HELPFUL HINTS

- String may be soaked in glue rather than drawn through it.

- Be sure the mixture of tempera is thin for this printing activity. You might want to start with a thicker mixture and test it with commercial stamps to ensure the proper consistency.

- Do not use string longer than 12 inches.

DEVELOPMENTAL GOALS

Develop creativity, small motor development, and hand-eye coordination; use familiar materials in new ways; learn the design concept of pattern.

PREPARATION

Discuss various kinds of stamps (e.g., stamps used to send letters, stamps for entry to a show). Discuss which kinds of designs and/or patterns the children could make as stamps.

PROCESS

1. Cover one side of the wood block with a thin coat of glue.
2. Deposit a small amount of glue on a piece of cardboard and pull the string through the glue.
3. Give the string an even coat of glue.
4. Place the string in the glue on the block so it forms a design.
5. Allow the block to dry thoroughly. Make sure the string does not overlap.
6. Paint the string on the block.
7. Lay the printing paper over several thicknesses of newspaper.
8. Press the block on a scrap of paper to eliminate any excess paint.
9. Several prints can be made from the printing paper before applying more paint.

VARIATIONS

- Instead of painting the design, make a print by stamping on an ink pad.
- Make original stationery by stamping several sheets of paper with the stamp.
- Vary the colors of paint between printings. When one color runs dry after several prints, dip the stamp in another color for new prints.
- Make initialed stationery by stamping letters onto pieces of paper. Remember that the letters must be backward on the stamp to appear correctly on the print.

NOTES FOR NEXT TIME: _____

_____

Recycled Puzzle Prints

MATERIALS

- ☐ old puzzle pieces
- ☐ white glue
- ☐ cereal box cardboard
- ☐ scissors
- ☐ tempera paint
- ☐ paintbrush
- ☐ paper
- ☐ construction paper

 **HELPFUL HINTS**

- Garage or yard sales are good sources of inexpensive puzzles. Also, ask friends to save puzzles with missing pieces.

- You may use a small trim paint roller and printer's ink instead of tempera paint. Water-based printing ink can be purchased from any art-supply store or educational-supply store. It can be used for any of the print-making activities in this book.

- If the tempera paint is too thin, thicken it with some regular household flour or even white glue.

DEVELOPMENTAL GOALS

Develop creativity, small motor development, and hand-eye coordination; use familiar objects in new ways; recycle puzzle pieces and learn the design concept of pattern.

PREPARATION

Talk about print making and how you can make several of the same image. Discuss what a pattern is—a repeat design. Talk about how patterns can be made of repeated lines of the same object (e.g., lines with alternating objects). Cut cereal boxes into pieces about 6" × 8".

PROCESS

1. Take several puzzle pieces and arrange them on the nonprinted side of the cereal box cardboard.

2. The pieces can be arranged to create a picture, a random design, or a pattern.

3. Once happy with the way the pieces look, glue them down and let the glue dry for an hour or so.

4. Use a paintbrush to cover the puzzle pieces with paint.

5. Lay a sheet of paper on top of the painted puzzle pieces.

6. Rub gently with the palm of the hand.

7. Peel off the paper to see the print.

VARIATIONS

- Repeat the process with a different color of ink. There may be some color mixing!

- Glue other objects to the puzzle print pattern, such as small twigs, beads, and cut-out pieces of Styrofoam. Repaint the design and print again.

NOTES FOR NEXT TIME: _____

_____

Copyright © 2004, Delmar Learning

4

Years Old and Up

Sandpaper Rubbings

MATERIALS

- ☐ different grades of sand paper
- ☐ scissors
- ☐ crayons
- ☐ paper
- ☐ tempera paint
- ☐ paintbrushes

 **HELPFUL HINT**

- Shapes can be torn from sand-paper if children do not yet use scissors.

DEVELOPMENTAL GOALS

Develop creativity, small motor development, and hand-eye coordination; use familiar materials in new ways; and learn the design concepts of line and pattern.

PREPARATION

Talk about the different textures of the sandpaper. Let the children feel each kind of sandpaper.

PROCESS

1. Cut the sandpaper into different shapes.
2. Put the paper over the sandpaper shape.
3. Color over the sandpaper with crayons.
4. Each grade of sandpaper will make a different texture.

VARIATIONS

- Paint over the sandpaper shape. Press it onto a piece of paper to make a print.
- Cut the sandpaper into letters.
- Make a sandpaper A. Do a crayon rubbing of it. Draw pictures of things that start with the letter A around the printed letter A. Repeat with other letters.

NOTES FOR NEXT TIME: _____
_____
_____
_____

Spatter Prints on Fabric

MATERIALS

- [ ] washable fabric (e.g., old sheet, piece of burlap, or unbleached muslin)
- [ ] 1/4 cup liquid dye or 1/2 package of powdered dye in 1 pint of hot water
- [ ] bowls
- [ ] mixing spoon
- [ ] paintbrushes (or toothbrushes)
- [ ] craft sticks (or old combs)
- [ ] small, shallow containers (cut-down 1/2 pint milk containers work well)

💡 HELPFUL HINTS

- If the fabric is to be used as a covering, brush or spray on a protective coat of clear shellac.
- Do this in a well-ventilated area, preferably outdoors.
- Do not use spatter-dyed fabric for articles that directly contact other articles (e.g., pillow covers), because the dye may rub off.
- An adult should mix the dye.
- Mix a bit of liquid soap into the dye mixture to make clean up easier on the hands.

DEVELOPMENTAL GOALS

Develop creativity, small motor development, and hand-eye coordination and learn the design concept of pattern.

PREPARATION

Mix liquid or powdered dye. Put the dye mixture in the small, shallow containers.

PROCESS

LIQUID DYE

1. Place the material on a flat surface with newspapers around the work area.
2. Dip a toothbrush or paintbrush in dye.
3. Run a comb or craft stick across the brush, making dye spatters.
4. Continue spattering a design onto the fabric.
5. Use two or three colors for interesting patterns.
6. Allow the fabric to dry.

VARIATIONS

- Use liquid tempera paint instead of dye if the fabric will not be washed.
- Spatter paint around cut-out construction paper designs.

NOTES FOR NEXT TIME: _____

_____

_____

Copyright © 2004, Delmar Learning

Sponge Prints

MATERIALS

- ☐ sponges
- ☐ scissors
- ☐ liquid tempera paint in shallow container (aluminum pie tins work well)
- ☐ paper

 **HELPFUL HINTS**

- Some children may not want to get their fingers in the paint. Let them hold the sponge with a spring-type clothespin, then print.

- The younger the printer, the fewer the shapes required for printing. These children are at the stage where they are just learning the process. With fewer choices with which to print, they can better concentrate on the process.

DEVELOPMENTAL GOALS

Develop creativity, small motor development, and hand-eye coordination; use familiar objects in new ways; and learn the design concept of pattern.

PREPARATION

Cut sponges into a variety of sizes and shapes.

PROCESS

1. Dip the sponge pieces in tempera paint.
2. Apply the sponge to paper to print.
3. Continue printing to make an overall pattern.
4. Print one line of one shape, another line with a different shape.
5. Print in zigzag lines and vertical or horizontal lines.

VARIATIONS

- Soak the paper in water. Lay the wet paper on a smooth surface and remove all the wrinkles and excess water. Print on the moist paper for a softer, blurry-type print.
- Print with several different colors of paint.
- Print on different kinds of paper, such as tissue, construction paper, cardboard, and pieces of white gift boxes.

NOTES FOR NEXT TIME: _____

_____

_____

_____

Spray Prints

MATERIALS

- ☐ construction paper
- ☐ scissors
- ☐ large sheets of white construction paper
- ☐ spray bottles
- ☐ tempera paint
- ☐ small rocks to use as weights

💡 HELPFUL HINTS

- Plan an outdoor walk to gather the small stones to use as weights in this activity.
- Be sure you check that the spray bottle is not clogged before filling it with paint.
- Because the spray covers a wide area, the larger the sheet of paper the better for this activity.

DEVELOPMENTAL GOALS

Develop creativity, small motor development, and hand-eye coordination and learn the design concepts of pattern, shape, and placement.

PREPARATION

Mix a thin solution of tempera paint. Pour the paint into a plastic spray bottle. Set a small funnel over the spray bottle to make this easier to do.

PROCESS

1. Cut or tear shapes out of construction paper.
2. Arrange the cut-out shapes in some design or pattern over the sheet of white construction paper.
3. Weigh down the shapes with the small rocks.
4. Spray the tempera paint lightly over the shape design.
5. When the paint has dried, pick up the shapes to discover the designs underneath.

VARIATIONS

- Use crayons or markers to complete the design after the paint is dried.
- Use heavy-weight washers to hold down the shapes while spraying around them.
- Use different colors of construction paper for the background.
- Very young children enjoy just spraying paint without the shapes
- Use several colors of paint for spraying.

NOTES FOR NEXT TIME: _____

_____

Copyright © 2004, Delmar Learning

Stick Prints

MATERIALS

- ☐ small sticks, 2 to 3 inches long, of various sizes and shapes
- ☐ tempera paint
- ☐ brush
- ☐ paper
- ☐ pad of newspaper

HELPFUL HINTS

- Beginning printers do not need to make drawings first. They can simply print with the stick in any fashion they choose.
- Go outdoors and have the children collect the sticks for this activity. It is much more fun than collecting them yourself!
- Older children may enjoy making mosaic effects with stick printing. This is done by leaving a narrow space of background paper between each print.

DEVELOPMENTAL GOALS

Develop creativity, small motor development, and hand-eye coordination and learn the design concepts of pattern and placement.

PREPARATION

Cut a number of sticks of different sizes and shapes, 2 or 3 inches long, making sure the ends are cut straight.

PROCESS

1. Make a light pencil drawing or design on paper.
2. Mix a small amount of paint on a piece of nonabsorbent scrap paper and smooth it with a brush to an even consistency.
3. Dip the stick in the paint.
4. Press the stick to a scrap of paper and print one or two images to remove any excess paint.
5. Press the stick to the drawing/design that has been placed on a pad of newspaper and repeat printing with the stick until the image becomes too light.
6. Repeat the process until the picture/design is complete.

VARIATIONS

- Things like jar lids and matchbox folders are also possible printing tools for this activity.
- Unusual patterns may be created by dipping the edges of any of the objects in paint.
- Interesting effects can be created by overlapping individual prints and colors.
- Try twisting the stick when printing for a different effect.
- Vary colors when printing with the stick.
- Use different shapes, colors, and kinds of paper.
- Use printing designs for wrapping paper, placemats, and box covers.

NOTES FOR NEXT TIME: _____

_____

Styrofoam Tray Prints

MATERIALS

- ☐ Styrofoam tray
- ☐ tempera paint
- ☐ small paint rollers (the kind used for painting trim)
- ☐ rolling pin
- ☐ paper or fabric
- ☐ pen or pencil
- ☐ shallow container for paint

💡 HELPFUL HINTS

- This activity is appropriate for children whose small motor skills are developed enough to handle the print roller.

- Allow the children using the roller for the first time to practice using the roller on scrap paper. Some children may enjoy just using the roller itself!

- When using recycled Styrofoam trays, be sure to wash the trays in bleach before using them. Do not use Styrofoam trays that were used to hold meat.

DEVELOPMENTAL GOALS

Develop creativity, small motor development, hand-eye coordination and learn the design concepts of pattern, line, and size.

PREPARATION

Talk about how repeating a design makes a pattern. Discuss the types of designs the children might like to make. Explain that the idea of this activity is to create a design on the tray by indenting a pen or a pencil into the tray.

PROCESS

1. Give each child a Styrofoam tray.
2. Use a pen or a pencil to make a design in the Styrofoam. Press hard enough to dent the Styrofoam.
3. Remember that letters print reversed, so if the children want letters they must draw them backward.
4. After the design is complete, roll ink evenly onto the tray.
5. Place a piece of paper on the ink.
6. Use a rolling pin to help transfer the design onto the paper.
7. Carefully, lift the paper evenly. There is the print.

VARIATIONS

- Use different kinds of paper, such as brown wrapping paper, newsprint, construction paper, and classified ads.
- Use different colors of ink.

NOTES FOR NEXT TIME: _____

_____

_____

_____

Copyright © 2004, Delmar Learning

Texture Prints

DEVELOPMENTAL GOALS

Develop creativity, small motor development, hand-eye coordination and learn the design concept of pattern.

PREPARATION

Talk with the children about how things look and feel. Use the word *texture* in your discussion. Discuss the items collected for this activity and how each looks and feels.

PROCESS

1. Give each child a piece of paper and a shallow container filled with paint.
2. Challenge each child to print with as many differently textured items as they can.
3. Encourage the children to repeat prints to create patterns.

VARIATIONS

- Use different colors of paint with the same object.
- Use different objects with the same color of paint.
- Print in a zigzag pattern, a vertical line, and in a horizontal line. Alternate colors in any of these patterns.

NOTES FOR NEXT TIME: _____

_____

_____

_____

MATERIALS

- ☐ materials with interesting textures such as cardboard
- ☐ sandpaper
- ☐ bristle brushes
- ☐ wadded cloth
- ☐ burlap
- ☐ paper
- ☐ paint in small, shallow containers

💡 HELPFUL HINTS

- With very young children, demonstrate the printing process initially (dip the object in paint, press the object onto the paper). Do this once and only once.

- Let the children experiment on their own from there.

- With beginning printers, it is generally best to use one color of paint. This allows the printers to concentrate on the process and avoid distraction by the number of colors.

Copyright © 2004, Delmar Learning

Try These—Experiments with Color

DEVELOPMENTAL GOALS

To develop creativity, small motor development, and hand-eye coordination and learn the design concepts of pattern, tone, and contrast.

MATERIALS

- ☐ paint
- ☐ printing objects
- ☐ paper (see following for specifics)

💡 HELPFUL HINT

- Recycled muffin tins work well using different consistencies of paint. Each muffin tin compartment can hold a different thickness or type of paint.

NOTES FOR NEXT TIME:

_____

_____

_____

_____

_____

_____

PREPARATION

First, read the following "Process" section. Then, prepare the paint and gather the kind of paper needed for the printing variation.

PROCESS

1. Alternate thin transparent watercolor with thick tempera paint when printing with objects.

2. Use a light color to print on dark paper or vice versa.

3. Use thin, transparent paint on colored paper or cloth so that the color of the background shows through.

4. Combine two objects of the same shape and size and use a different color for each.

5. Combine objects of different sizes and shapes, using a different color for each.

6. Vary the amount of paint used—heavier amounts make deeper colors, lesser amounts make lighter colors.

VARIATIONS

- Dip the object in two colors of paint and see how the colors mix.
- Use one of the preceding color variations on newspaper classified ads.
- Use printed paper for book covers for stories, poems, pictures, and notes.
- Use printed paper for place cards, gift wrapping, and gift-container covers.

Copyright © 2004, Delmar Learning

Try These—Experiments with Pattern

3 Years Old and Up

MATERIALS

- ☐ paper
- ☐ printing objects of your choice
- ☐ paint in shallow containers

💡 HELPFUL HINTS

- Beginning printers will probably be able to do overall-pattern prints.

- Encourage experienced printers to create their own patterns.

NOTES FOR NEXT TIME:

_____

_____

_____

_____

_____

_____

DEVELOPMENTAL GOALS

Develop creativity, small motor development, and hand-eye coordination and learn the design concept of pattern.

PREPARATION

Talk about pattern—how it is made by repeating a design. Give each child a large piece of paper, access to shallow containers of paint, and objects to print.

PROCESS

1. Suggest printing a design in the following ways.

2. Print a shape in straight rows or zigzags. Repeat the design to create an all-over pattern.

3. Use a different shape for each row and add a second color in alternate rows.

4. Group shapes in units of two or three and print a rhythmic design. Move shapes to alternate positions and print in a second color.

5. Print in a border design with one shape or group of shapes in a regular, repeated manner.

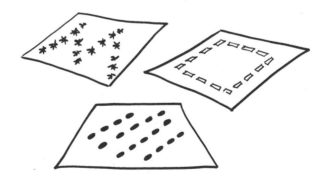

VARIATIONS

- Use different kinds of paper, such as cardboard, tissue and brown wrapping paper.

- Dip objects in one, then another color. See how the colors mix.

- Use the border prints for things like writing paper and place mats.

Copyright © 2004, Delmar Learning

PRINT MAKING 43

Vegetable Prints

MATERIALS

- ☐ firm vegetables such as potatoes and carrots
- ☐ plastic knife
- ☐ shallow containers of paint
- ☐ paper for printing

💡 HELPFUL HINTS

- This is a good activity for vegetables that are getting old. Even limp vegetables are still good for printing. In fact, vegetables are easier to carve when they are not fresh.
- Encourage children to identify different vegetables for print making. How about rutabaga or turnips?

DEVELOPMENTAL GOALS

Develop creativity, small motor development, and hand-eye coordination and learn the design concepts of pattern and line.

PREPARATION

Carve a simple design into the vegetable by notching the edges or carving holes with a small, plastic knife. Talk about pattern with the children. Discuss how a pattern has the same object repeated in different lines.

PROCESS

1. Give each child a potato for printing.
2. Let older children carve the potato for printing.
3. For younger children, carve a simple design in the potato.
4. Dip the potato in the paint.
5. Press the potato onto paper to make a print.
6. Encourage the children to make patterns by printing lines, swirls, zigzags, and so on.

VARIATIONS

- Instead of food, carve out pieces of packaging Styrofoam for this activity.
- Have several colors of paint with which to print.
- Use different kinds of paper to print on, such as newspaper want ads, cardboard pieces, and brown wrapping paper.
- Use the print to wrap gifts for parents and friends.

NOTES FOR NEXT TIME: _____

_____

_____

_____

Copyright © 2004, Delmar Learning

3 Years Old and UP

Weed Prints

MATERIALS

- ☐ a variety of weeds
- ☐ paper
- ☐ tempera paint in shallow containers.

 **HELPFUL HINTS**

- If the weeds get too dry, they will not print as well.
- Be sure children do not have allergies to any of the weeds used in this activity.

DEVELOPMENTAL GOALS

Develop creativity, small motor development, and hand-eye coordination and appreciate pattern and beauty in nature.

PREPARATION

Go on a walk and collect weeds for printing. Weeds in flower (e.g., golden-rod, Queen Anne's lace) generally work best.

PROCESS

1. Give each child a piece of paper.
2. Dip the top (flowering part) into paint.
3. Press the weed onto the paper.
4. Continue dipping and printing with the weeds until a design and/or pattern emerges.

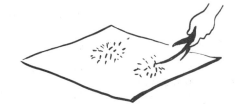

VARIATION

- Print with other natural objects, such as small stones and twigs added to the printed weed design.

NOTES FOR NEXT TIME: _____
_____
_____
_____

Copyright © 2004, Delmar Learning

What Can It Be?

MATERIALS

- ☐ long pieces of newsprint paper (18" × 24") (or classified ads from the newspaper)
- ☐ tempera paint in shallow pan (cookie sheets work well)
- ☐ crayons
- ☐ markers
- ☐ pail of soapy water
- ☐ paper towels

💡 HELPFUL HINTS

- Toddlers will enjoy the simple process of printing without making prints.
- The more foot and hand prints, the more chances for creating.
- This is a fun activity to do outdoors where there are fewer worries about mess and cleanup.

DEVELOPMENTAL GOALS

Develop creativity, small motor development, and hand-eye coordination and create designs from foot and hand prints.

PREPARATION

Cover the floor by taping down newspapers. Tape long sheets of paper onto newspapers.

PROCESS

1. Have the child step into a pan of paint and put the hands in the paint.
2. Step out of the paint onto the paper to make foot and hand prints.
3. Let the prints dry completely.
4. Using crayons and markers, use the foot and hand prints to make a design or any kind of original creation.
5. Give the children some ideas to get them started (e.g., foot "people," hand "trees," foot "animals").

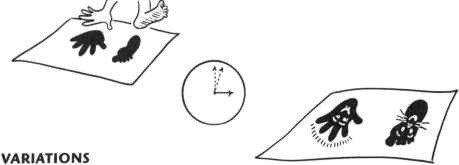

VARIATIONS

- Use other body parts to make prints, like elbows, forearms, and knees. Make designs and pictures with these prints.
- For children who do not want to get messy, trace around the children's shoes onto pieces of paper. Then, let the children use crayons or markers to make anything they choose.

NOTES FOR NEXT TIME: _____

_____

Copyright © 2004, Delmar Learning

A

Wheelies!

MATERIALS

- ☐ liquid tempera paint
- ☐ liquid starch
- ☐ cookie sheet or tray with sides
- ☐ paintbrush for mixing
- ☐ small wheel toys (cars, trucks, etc.)
- ☐ large sheets of paper

 **HELPFUL HINT**

- This activity inspires even the most reluctant artists. It is fun, messy, and uses toys that are familiar to most children.

DEVELOPMENTAL GOALS

Develop creativity, small motor development, and hand-eye coordination and use familiar materials in new ways.

PREPARATION

Pour a big glob of liquid starch onto the cookie sheet or tray. Put a big spoonful of paint in the starch glob. Mix the paint and starch with a paintbrush.

PROCESS

1. Have the child choose a small wheel toy.
2. Roll the toy through the paint.
3. Drive the car over a piece of paper, making designs and tracks.
4. Use other wheel toys to roll through the paint and over the paper.
5. Let the painting dry completely.

VARIATIONS

- Use different colors of paint in the tray. This way colors will mix both in the tray and on the paper.
- Have the children bring small wheel toys from home for this activity.
- Use a stamp pad to wheel over. Then, roll the wheel onto the paper.
- Tape paper to the wall near the floor and paint source. Wheel the paint-dipped toy up and down on the paper.

NOTES FOR NEXT TIME: _____

_____

_____

_____

Wood-Block and String Prints

MATERIALS

- ☐ wooden block
- ☐ string
- ☐ paste or glue
- ☐ paper
- ☐ tempera paint
- ☐ brush

💡 HELPFUL HINT

- Make the first print on scrap paper to eliminate any excess paint.

NOTES FOR NEXT TIME:

_____

_____

_____

_____

_____

DEVELOPMENTAL GOALS

Develop creativity, small motor development, and hand-eye coordination and learn the design concepts of pattern and repeated images.

PREPARATION

Discuss which designs children would like to make. Explain that these designs will be made with string.

PROCESS

1. Coat the entire length of the string with paste or glue.

2. While the string is still wet, wrap it around the wooden block to form a design.

3. Place a small amount of tempera paint on a piece of scrap paper, and smooth it with a brush to an even consistency.

4. Choose the side of the string-wrapped block that has the most pleasing design.

5. Dip that side into the paint, or apply the paint to the string with a brush.

6. Lift the block from the paint, and press it against the paper with some pressure.

7. Several prints can be made before applying more paint.

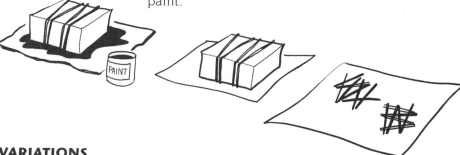

VARIATIONS

- Make all-over patterns by alternating the sides of the block in printing.
- Make wrapping paper using wood-block and string printing.
- Use different colors of paint.

Copyright © 2004, Delmar Learning

Yarn Prints

MATERIALS

- ☐ yarn
- ☐ glue
- ☐ scissors
- ☐ cardboard or oaktag
- ☐ paper
- ☐ tempera paint
- ☐ crayons

💡 HELPFUL HINTS

- The thicker the yarn, the better the print.
- Thin the glue with a little water so it runs easily from the container.

NOTES FOR NEXT TIME:

_____

_____

_____

_____

DEVELOPMENTAL GOALS

Develop creativity, small motor development, and hand-eye coordination; use familiar materials in new ways and learn the design concepts of pattern and line.

PREPARATION

Talk about how designs can be repeated to make patterns. Discuss how lines can be zigzag, horizontal, vertical, and so on.

PROCESS

1. Use crayons to draw a pattern, design, or picture on the cardboard.
2. Outline parts or all of the picture with glue.
3. Apply glue to the yarn.
4. Let the yarn and glue dry thoroughly.
5. Brush tempera paint over the picture.
6. Place another piece of paper over the picture.
7. Press lightly with the palm of the hand.
8. Peel off the paper to see the string print!

VARIATIONS

- Use thinner yarn, string, or even rope to outline the design.
- Draw a simple object with crayons onto a square piece of cardboard about 4" × 4". Glue yarn around the object. Let it dry. Print with it on paper to make original stationery.

Copyright © 2004, Delmar Learning

Index by Ages

ALL AGES

ABCs and 123s 1
Apple Prints. 2
Berry Nice Prints. 4
Bubble Prints 5
Can-Top Prints 6
Circle Challenge 9
Creative Shoe Prints 14
Finger Paint Prints 16
Finger Prints 17
Great Balls of Fun! 20
Hair's the Thing. 21
Hand and Foot Prints 22
Kitchen Prints 23
Pine Cone Prints. 29
Plunge into It! 31
Print All Over—Body Part Prints 32
Sponge Prints 37
Spray Prints. 38
Stick Prints. 39
Texture Prints 41
Vegetable Prints 44
What Can It Be? 46
Wheelies! 47

4 YEARS AND UP

Background Paper Experiments. 3
Cardboard Relief Prints 8
First Experiments with Monoprints 18
Glue and Leaf Prints 19
Monoprints One More Time! 24
Monoprints—Even One More Way! 25
Nature Spatter Prints. 26
Printing Stamps 33
Sandpaper Rubbings 35
Try These—Experiments with Color 42
Yarn Prints 49

5 YEARS AND UP

Cardboard or Rubber Block Prints 7
Cloth Prints 10
Crayon Prints. 12
Crayon Shavings Prints 13
Paint Monoprints 27
Spatter Prints on Fabric. 36
Wood-Block and String Prints 48

3 YEARS AND UP

Cork Prints 11
Dip It! 15
Pasta Prints 28
Play Dough Printing 30
Recycled Puzzle Prints 34
Styrofoam Tray Prints 40
Try These—Experiments with Pattern 43
Weed Prints 45